# MY PASSWORD JOURNAL

# PASSWORD ORGANIZER

| WEBSITE | WEBSITE |
| --- | --- |
| | |
| USERNAME | USERNAME |
| PASSWORD | PASSWORD |

| WEBSITE | WEBSITE |
| --- | --- |
| | |
| USERNAME | USERNAME |
| PASSWORD | PASSWORD |

| WEBSITE | WEBSITE |
| --- | --- |
| | |
| USERNAME | USERNAME |
| PASSWORD | PASSWORD |

| WEBSITE | WEBSITE |
| --- | --- |
| | |
| USERNAME | USERNAME |
| PASSWORD | PASSWORD |

| WEBSITE | WEBSITE |
| --- | --- |
| | |
| USERNAME | USERNAME |
| PASSWORD | PASSWORD |

| WEBSITE | WEBSITE |
| --- | --- |
| | |
| USERNAME | USERNAME |
| PASSWORD | PASSWORD |

| WEBSITE | WEBSITE |
| --- | --- |
| | |
| USERNAME | USERNAME |
| PASSWORD | PASSWORD |

| WEBSITE | WEBSITE |
| --- | --- |
| | |
| USERNAME | USERNAME |
| PASSWORD | PASSWORD |

# PASSWORD ORGANIZER

| WEBSITE | WEBSITE |
|---|---|
| | |
| USERNAME | USERNAME |
| PASSWORD | PASSWORD |

| WEBSITE | WEBSITE |
|---|---|
| | |
| USERNAME | USERNAME |
| PASSWORD | PASSWORD |

| WEBSITE | WEBSITE |
|---|---|
| | |
| USERNAME | USERNAME |
| PASSWORD | PASSWORD |

| WEBSITE | WEBSITE |
|---|---|
| | |
| USERNAME | USERNAME |
| PASSWORD | PASSWORD |

| WEBSITE | WEBSITE |
|---|---|
| | |
| USERNAME | USERNAME |
| PASSWORD | PASSWORD |

| WEBSITE | WEBSITE |
|---|---|
| | |
| USERNAME | USERNAME |
| PASSWORD | PASSWORD |

| WEBSITE | WEBSITE |
|---|---|
| | |
| USERNAME | USERNAME |
| PASSWORD | PASSWORD |

| WEBSITE | WEBSITE |
|---|---|
| | |
| USERNAME | USERNAME |
| PASSWORD | PASSWORD |

# PASSWORD ORGANIZER

| WEBSITE | WEBSITE |
|---|---|
| | |
| USERNAME | USERNAME |
| PASSWORD | PASSWORD |

| WEBSITE | WEBSITE |
|---|---|
| | |
| USERNAME | USERNAME |
| PASSWORD | PASSWORD |

| WEBSITE | WEBSITE |
|---|---|
| | |
| USERNAME | USERNAME |
| PASSWORD | PASSWORD |

| WEBSITE | WEBSITE |
|---|---|
| | |
| USERNAME | USERNAME |
| PASSWORD | PASSWORD |

| WEBSITE | WEBSITE |
|---|---|
| | |
| USERNAME | USERNAME |
| PASSWORD | PASSWORD |

| WEBSITE | WEBSITE |
|---|---|
| | |
| USERNAME | USERNAME |
| PASSWORD | PASSWORD |

| WEBSITE | WEBSITE |
|---|---|
| | |
| USERNAME | USERNAME |
| PASSWORD | PASSWORD |

| WEBSITE | WEBSITE |
|---|---|
| | |
| USERNAME | USERNAME |
| PASSWORD | PASSWORD |

# PASSWORD ORGANIZER

| WEBSITE | WEBSITE |
|---|---|
| | |
| USERNAME | USERNAME |
| PASSWORD | PASSWORD |

| WEBSITE | WEBSITE |
|---|---|
| | |
| USERNAME | USERNAME |
| PASSWORD | PASSWORD |

| WEBSITE | WEBSITE |
|---|---|
| | |
| USERNAME | USERNAME |
| PASSWORD | PASSWORD |

| WEBSITE | WEBSITE |
|---|---|
| | |
| USERNAME | USERNAME |
| PASSWORD | PASSWORD |

| WEBSITE | WEBSITE |
|---|---|
| | |
| USERNAME | USERNAME |
| PASSWORD | PASSWORD |

| WEBSITE | WEBSITE |
|---|---|
| | |
| USERNAME | USERNAME |
| PASSWORD | PASSWORD |

| WEBSITE | WEBSITE |
|---|---|
| | |
| USERNAME | USERNAME |
| PASSWORD | PASSWORD |

| WEBSITE | WEBSITE |
|---|---|
| | |
| USERNAME | USERNAME |
| PASSWORD | PASSWORD |

# PASSWORD ORGANIZER

| WEBSITE | WEBSITE |
|---|---|
| | |
| USERNAME | USERNAME |
| PASSWORD | PASSWORD |

| WEBSITE | WEBSITE |
|---|---|
| | |
| USERNAME | USERNAME |
| PASSWORD | PASSWORD |

| WEBSITE | WEBSITE |
|---|---|
| | |
| USERNAME | USERNAME |
| PASSWORD | PASSWORD |

| WEBSITE | WEBSITE |
|---|---|
| | |
| USERNAME | USERNAME |
| PASSWORD | PASSWORD |

| WEBSITE | WEBSITE |
|---|---|
| | |
| USERNAME | USERNAME |
| PASSWORD | PASSWORD |

| WEBSITE | WEBSITE |
|---|---|
| | |
| USERNAME | USERNAME |
| PASSWORD | PASSWORD |

| WEBSITE | WEBSITE |
|---|---|
| | |
| USERNAME | USERNAME |
| PASSWORD | PASSWORD |

| WEBSITE | WEBSITE |
|---|---|
| | |
| USERNAME | USERNAME |
| PASSWORD | PASSWORD |

# PASSWORD ORGANIZER

| WEBSITE | | WEBSITE |
|---|---|---|
| | | |
| USERNAME | | USERNAME |
| PASSWORD | | PASSWORD |

| WEBSITE | | WEBSITE |
|---|---|---|
| | | |
| USERNAME | | USERNAME |
| PASSWORD | | PASSWORD |

| WEBSITE | | WEBSITE |
|---|---|---|
| | | |
| USERNAME | | USERNAME |
| PASSWORD | | PASSWORD |

| WEBSITE | | WEBSITE |
|---|---|---|
| | | |
| USERNAME | | USERNAME |
| PASSWORD | | PASSWORD |

| WEBSITE | | WEBSITE |
|---|---|---|
| | | |
| USERNAME | | USERNAME |
| PASSWORD | | PASSWORD |

| WEBSITE | | WEBSITE |
|---|---|---|
| | | |
| USERNAME | | USERNAME |
| PASSWORD | | PASSWORD |

| WEBSITE | | WEBSITE |
|---|---|---|
| | | |
| USERNAME | | USERNAME |
| PASSWORD | | PASSWORD |

| WEBSITE | | WEBSITE |
|---|---|---|
| | | |
| USERNAME | | USERNAME |
| PASSWORD | | PASSWORD |

# PASSWORD ORGANIZER

| WEBSITE | | WEBSITE | |
|---|---|---|---|
| USERNAME | | USERNAME | |
| PASSWORD | | PASSWORD | |

| WEBSITE | | WEBSITE | |
|---|---|---|---|
| USERNAME | | USERNAME | |
| PASSWORD | | PASSWORD | |

| WEBSITE | | WEBSITE | |
|---|---|---|---|
| USERNAME | | USERNAME | |
| PASSWORD | | PASSWORD | |

| WEBSITE | | WEBSITE | |
|---|---|---|---|
| USERNAME | | USERNAME | |
| PASSWORD | | PASSWORD | |

| WEBSITE | | WEBSITE | |
|---|---|---|---|
| USERNAME | | USERNAME | |
| PASSWORD | | PASSWORD | |

| WEBSITE | | WEBSITE | |
|---|---|---|---|
| USERNAME | | USERNAME | |
| PASSWORD | | PASSWORD | |

| WEBSITE | | WEBSITE | |
|---|---|---|---|
| USERNAME | | USERNAME | |
| PASSWORD | | PASSWORD | |

| WEBSITE | | WEBSITE | |
|---|---|---|---|
| USERNAME | | USERNAME | |
| PASSWORD | | PASSWORD | |

# PASSWORD ORGANIZER

| WEBSITE | | WEBSITE | |
|---|---|---|---|
| USERNAME | | USERNAME | |
| PASSWORD | | PASSWORD | |

| WEBSITE | | WEBSITE | |
|---|---|---|---|
| USERNAME | | USERNAME | |
| PASSWORD | | PASSWORD | |

| WEBSITE | | WEBSITE | |
|---|---|---|---|
| USERNAME | | USERNAME | |
| PASSWORD | | PASSWORD | |

| WEBSITE | | WEBSITE | |
|---|---|---|---|
| USERNAME | | USERNAME | |
| PASSWORD | | PASSWORD | |

| WEBSITE | | WEBSITE | |
|---|---|---|---|
| USERNAME | | USERNAME | |
| PASSWORD | | PASSWORD | |

| WEBSITE | | WEBSITE | |
|---|---|---|---|
| USERNAME | | USERNAME | |
| PASSWORD | | PASSWORD | |

| WEBSITE | | WEBSITE | |
|---|---|---|---|
| USERNAME | | USERNAME | |
| PASSWORD | | PASSWORD | |

| WEBSITE | | WEBSITE | |
|---|---|---|---|
| USERNAME | | USERNAME | |
| PASSWORD | | PASSWORD | |

# PASSWORD ORGANIZER

| WEBSITE | WEBSITE |
|---|---|
| | |
| USERNAME | USERNAME |
| PASSWORD | PASSWORD |

| WEBSITE | WEBSITE |
|---|---|
| | |
| USERNAME | USERNAME |
| PASSWORD | PASSWORD |

| WEBSITE | WEBSITE |
|---|---|
| | |
| USERNAME | USERNAME |
| PASSWORD | PASSWORD |

| WEBSITE | WEBSITE |
|---|---|
| | |
| USERNAME | USERNAME |
| PASSWORD | PASSWORD |

| WEBSITE | WEBSITE |
|---|---|
| | |
| USERNAME | USERNAME |
| PASSWORD | PASSWORD |

| WEBSITE | WEBSITE |
|---|---|
| | |
| USERNAME | USERNAME |
| PASSWORD | PASSWORD |

| WEBSITE | WEBSITE |
|---|---|
| | |
| USERNAME | USERNAME |
| PASSWORD | PASSWORD |

| WEBSITE | WEBSITE |
|---|---|
| | |
| USERNAME | USERNAME |
| PASSWORD | PASSWORD |

# PASSWORD ORGANIZER

| WEBSITE | WEBSITE |
|---|---|
| | |
| USERNAME | USERNAME |
| PASSWORD | PASSWORD |

| WEBSITE | WEBSITE |
|---|---|
| | |
| USERNAME | USERNAME |
| PASSWORD | PASSWORD |

| WEBSITE | WEBSITE |
|---|---|
| | |
| USERNAME | USERNAME |
| PASSWORD | PASSWORD |

| WEBSITE | WEBSITE |
|---|---|
| | |
| USERNAME | USERNAME |
| PASSWORD | PASSWORD |

| WEBSITE | WEBSITE |
|---|---|
| | |
| USERNAME | USERNAME |
| PASSWORD | PASSWORD |

| WEBSITE | WEBSITE |
|---|---|
| | |
| USERNAME | USERNAME |
| PASSWORD | PASSWORD |

| WEBSITE | WEBSITE |
|---|---|
| | |
| USERNAME | USERNAME |
| PASSWORD | PASSWORD |

| WEBSITE | WEBSITE |
|---|---|
| | |
| USERNAME | USERNAME |
| PASSWORD | PASSWORD |

# PASSWORD ORGANIZER

| WEBSITE | | WEBSITE | |
|---|---|---|---|
| | | | |
| USERNAME | | USERNAME | |
| PASSWORD | | PASSWORD | |

| WEBSITE | | WEBSITE | |
|---|---|---|---|
| | | | |
| USERNAME | | USERNAME | |
| PASSWORD | | PASSWORD | |

| WEBSITE | | WEBSITE | |
|---|---|---|---|
| | | | |
| USERNAME | | USERNAME | |
| PASSWORD | | PASSWORD | |

| WEBSITE | | WEBSITE | |
|---|---|---|---|
| | | | |
| USERNAME | | USERNAME | |
| PASSWORD | | PASSWORD | |

| WEBSITE | | WEBSITE | |
|---|---|---|---|
| | | | |
| USERNAME | | USERNAME | |
| PASSWORD | | PASSWORD | |

| WEBSITE | | WEBSITE | |
|---|---|---|---|
| | | | |
| USERNAME | | USERNAME | |
| PASSWORD | | PASSWORD | |

| WEBSITE | | WEBSITE | |
|---|---|---|---|
| | | | |
| USERNAME | | USERNAME | |
| PASSWORD | | PASSWORD | |

| WEBSITE | | WEBSITE | |
|---|---|---|---|
| | | | |
| USERNAME | | USERNAME | |
| PASSWORD | | PASSWORD | |

# PASSWORD ORGANIZER

| WEBSITE | | WEBSITE | |
|---------|---|---------|---|
| USERNAME | | USERNAME | |
| PASSWORD | | PASSWORD | |

| WEBSITE | | WEBSITE | |
|---------|---|---------|---|
| USERNAME | | USERNAME | |
| PASSWORD | | PASSWORD | |

| WEBSITE | | WEBSITE | |
|---------|---|---------|---|
| USERNAME | | USERNAME | |
| PASSWORD | | PASSWORD | |

| WEBSITE | | WEBSITE | |
|---------|---|---------|---|
| USERNAME | | USERNAME | |
| PASSWORD | | PASSWORD | |

| WEBSITE | | WEBSITE | |
|---------|---|---------|---|
| USERNAME | | USERNAME | |
| PASSWORD | | PASSWORD | |

| WEBSITE | | WEBSITE | |
|---------|---|---------|---|
| USERNAME | | USERNAME | |
| PASSWORD | | PASSWORD | |

| WEBSITE | | WEBSITE | |
|---------|---|---------|---|
| USERNAME | | USERNAME | |
| PASSWORD | | PASSWORD | |

| WEBSITE | | WEBSITE | |
|---------|---|---------|---|
| USERNAME | | USERNAME | |
| PASSWORD | | PASSWORD | |

# PASSWORD ORGANIZER

| WEBSITE | WEBSITE |
|---|---|
| | |
| USERNAME | USERNAME |
| PASSWORD | PASSWORD |

| WEBSITE | WEBSITE |
|---|---|
| | |
| USERNAME | USERNAME |
| PASSWORD | PASSWORD |

| WEBSITE | WEBSITE |
|---|---|
| | |
| USERNAME | USERNAME |
| PASSWORD | PASSWORD |

| WEBSITE | WEBSITE |
|---|---|
| | |
| USERNAME | USERNAME |
| PASSWORD | PASSWORD |

| WEBSITE | WEBSITE |
|---|---|
| | |
| USERNAME | USERNAME |
| PASSWORD | PASSWORD |

| WEBSITE | WEBSITE |
|---|---|
| | |
| USERNAME | USERNAME |
| PASSWORD | PASSWORD |

| WEBSITE | WEBSITE |
|---|---|
| | |
| USERNAME | USERNAME |
| PASSWORD | PASSWORD |

| WEBSITE | WEBSITE |
|---|---|
| | |
| USERNAME | USERNAME |
| PASSWORD | PASSWORD |

# PASSWORD ORGANIZER

| WEBSITE | WEBSITE |
| --- | --- |
| | |
| USERNAME | USERNAME |
| PASSWORD | PASSWORD |

| WEBSITE | WEBSITE |
| --- | --- |
| | |
| USERNAME | USERNAME |
| PASSWORD | PASSWORD |

| WEBSITE | WEBSITE |
| --- | --- |
| | |
| USERNAME | USERNAME |
| PASSWORD | PASSWORD |

| WEBSITE | WEBSITE |
| --- | --- |
| | |
| USERNAME | USERNAME |
| PASSWORD | PASSWORD |

| WEBSITE | WEBSITE |
| --- | --- |
| | |
| USERNAME | USERNAME |
| PASSWORD | PASSWORD |

| WEBSITE | WEBSITE |
| --- | --- |
| | |
| USERNAME | USERNAME |
| PASSWORD | PASSWORD |

| WEBSITE | WEBSITE |
| --- | --- |
| | |
| USERNAME | USERNAME |
| PASSWORD | PASSWORD |

| WEBSITE | WEBSITE |
| --- | --- |
| | |
| USERNAME | USERNAME |
| PASSWORD | PASSWORD |

# PASSWORD ORGANIZER

| WEBSITE | | WEBSITE | |
|---|---|---|---|
| | | | |
| USERNAME | | USERNAME | |
| PASSWORD | | PASSWORD | |

| WEBSITE | | WEBSITE | |
|---|---|---|---|
| | | | |
| USERNAME | | USERNAME | |
| PASSWORD | | PASSWORD | |

| WEBSITE | | WEBSITE | |
|---|---|---|---|
| | | | |
| USERNAME | | USERNAME | |
| PASSWORD | | PASSWORD | |

| WEBSITE | | WEBSITE | |
|---|---|---|---|
| | | | |
| USERNAME | | USERNAME | |
| PASSWORD | | PASSWORD | |

| WEBSITE | | WEBSITE | |
|---|---|---|---|
| | | | |
| USERNAME | | USERNAME | |
| PASSWORD | | PASSWORD | |

| WEBSITE | | WEBSITE | |
|---|---|---|---|
| | | | |
| USERNAME | | USERNAME | |
| PASSWORD | | PASSWORD | |

| WEBSITE | | WEBSITE | |
|---|---|---|---|
| | | | |
| USERNAME | | USERNAME | |
| PASSWORD | | PASSWORD | |

| WEBSITE | | WEBSITE | |
|---|---|---|---|
| | | | |
| USERNAME | | USERNAME | |
| PASSWORD | | PASSWORD | |

# PASSWORD ORGANIZER

| WEBSITE | | WEBSITE | |
|---|---|---|---|
| USERNAME | | USERNAME | |
| PASSWORD | | PASSWORD | |

| WEBSITE | | WEBSITE | |
|---|---|---|---|
| USERNAME | | USERNAME | |
| PASSWORD | | PASSWORD | |

| WEBSITE | | WEBSITE | |
|---|---|---|---|
| USERNAME | | USERNAME | |
| PASSWORD | | PASSWORD | |

| WEBSITE | | WEBSITE | |
|---|---|---|---|
| USERNAME | | USERNAME | |
| PASSWORD | | PASSWORD | |

| WEBSITE | | WEBSITE | |
|---|---|---|---|
| USERNAME | | USERNAME | |
| PASSWORD | | PASSWORD | |

| WEBSITE | | WEBSITE | |
|---|---|---|---|
| USERNAME | | USERNAME | |
| PASSWORD | | PASSWORD | |

| WEBSITE | | WEBSITE | |
|---|---|---|---|
| USERNAME | | USERNAME | |
| PASSWORD | | PASSWORD | |

| WEBSITE | | WEBSITE | |
|---|---|---|---|
| USERNAME | | USERNAME | |
| PASSWORD | | PASSWORD | |

# PASSWORD ORGANIZER

| WEBSITE | WEBSITE |
|---|---|
| | |
| USERNAME | USERNAME |
| PASSWORD | PASSWORD |

| WEBSITE | WEBSITE |
|---|---|
| | |
| USERNAME | USERNAME |
| PASSWORD | PASSWORD |

| WEBSITE | WEBSITE |
|---|---|
| | |
| USERNAME | USERNAME |
| PASSWORD | PASSWORD |

| WEBSITE | WEBSITE |
|---|---|
| | |
| USERNAME | USERNAME |
| PASSWORD | PASSWORD |

| WEBSITE | WEBSITE |
|---|---|
| | |
| USERNAME | USERNAME |
| PASSWORD | PASSWORD |

| WEBSITE | WEBSITE |
|---|---|
| | |
| USERNAME | USERNAME |
| PASSWORD | PASSWORD |

| WEBSITE | WEBSITE |
|---|---|
| | |
| USERNAME | USERNAME |
| PASSWORD | PASSWORD |

| WEBSITE | WEBSITE |
|---|---|
| | |
| USERNAME | USERNAME |
| PASSWORD | PASSWORD |

# PASSWORD ORGANIZER

| WEBSITE | WEBSITE |
|---|---|
| | |
| USERNAME | USERNAME |
| PASSWORD | PASSWORD |

| WEBSITE | WEBSITE |
|---|---|
| | |
| USERNAME | USERNAME |
| PASSWORD | PASSWORD |

| WEBSITE | WEBSITE |
|---|---|
| | |
| USERNAME | USERNAME |
| PASSWORD | PASSWORD |

| WEBSITE | WEBSITE |
|---|---|
| | |
| USERNAME | USERNAME |
| PASSWORD | PASSWORD |

| WEBSITE | WEBSITE |
|---|---|
| | |
| USERNAME | USERNAME |
| PASSWORD | PASSWORD |

| WEBSITE | WEBSITE |
|---|---|
| | |
| USERNAME | USERNAME |
| PASSWORD | PASSWORD |

| WEBSITE | WEBSITE |
|---|---|
| | |
| USERNAME | USERNAME |
| PASSWORD | PASSWORD |

| WEBSITE | WEBSITE |
|---|---|
| | |
| USERNAME | USERNAME |
| PASSWORD | PASSWORD |

# PASSWORD ORGANIZER

| WEBSITE | WEBSITE |
|---|---|
| | |
| USERNAME | USERNAME |
| PASSWORD | PASSWORD |

| WEBSITE | WEBSITE |
|---|---|
| | |
| USERNAME | USERNAME |
| PASSWORD | PASSWORD |

| WEBSITE | WEBSITE |
|---|---|
| | |
| USERNAME | USERNAME |
| PASSWORD | PASSWORD |

| WEBSITE | WEBSITE |
|---|---|
| | |
| USERNAME | USERNAME |
| PASSWORD | PASSWORD |

| WEBSITE | WEBSITE |
|---|---|
| | |
| USERNAME | USERNAME |
| PASSWORD | PASSWORD |

| WEBSITE | WEBSITE |
|---|---|
| | |
| USERNAME | USERNAME |
| PASSWORD | PASSWORD |

| WEBSITE | WEBSITE |
|---|---|
| | |
| USERNAME | USERNAME |
| PASSWORD | PASSWORD |

| WEBSITE | WEBSITE |
|---|---|
| | |
| USERNAME | USERNAME |
| PASSWORD | PASSWORD |

# PASSWORD ORGANIZER

| WEBSITE | WEBSITE |
|---|---|
|  |  |
| USERNAME | USERNAME |
| PASSWORD | PASSWORD |

| WEBSITE | WEBSITE |
|---|---|
|  |  |
| USERNAME | USERNAME |
| PASSWORD | PASSWORD |

| WEBSITE | WEBSITE |
|---|---|
|  |  |
| USERNAME | USERNAME |
| PASSWORD | PASSWORD |

| WEBSITE | WEBSITE |
|---|---|
|  |  |
| USERNAME | USERNAME |
| PASSWORD | PASSWORD |

| WEBSITE | WEBSITE |
|---|---|
|  |  |
| USERNAME | USERNAME |
| PASSWORD | PASSWORD |

| WEBSITE | WEBSITE |
|---|---|
|  |  |
| USERNAME | USERNAME |
| PASSWORD | PASSWORD |

| WEBSITE | WEBSITE |
|---|---|
|  |  |
| USERNAME | USERNAME |
| PASSWORD | PASSWORD |

| WEBSITE | WEBSITE |
|---|---|
|  |  |
| USERNAME | USERNAME |
| PASSWORD | PASSWORD |

# PASSWORD ORGANIZER

| WEBSITE | WEBSITE |
|---------|---------|
| | |
| USERNAME | USERNAME |
| PASSWORD | PASSWORD |

| WEBSITE | WEBSITE |
|---------|---------|
| | |
| USERNAME | USERNAME |
| PASSWORD | PASSWORD |

| WEBSITE | WEBSITE |
|---------|---------|
| | |
| USERNAME | USERNAME |
| PASSWORD | PASSWORD |

| WEBSITE | WEBSITE |
|---------|---------|
| | |
| USERNAME | USERNAME |
| PASSWORD | PASSWORD |

| WEBSITE | WEBSITE |
|---------|---------|
| | |
| USERNAME | USERNAME |
| PASSWORD | PASSWORD |

| WEBSITE | WEBSITE |
|---------|---------|
| | |
| USERNAME | USERNAME |
| PASSWORD | PASSWORD |

| WEBSITE | WEBSITE |
|---------|---------|
| | |
| USERNAME | USERNAME |
| PASSWORD | PASSWORD |

| WEBSITE | WEBSITE |
|---------|---------|
| | |
| USERNAME | USERNAME |
| PASSWORD | PASSWORD |

# PASSWORD ORGANIZER

| WEBSITE | WEBSITE |
|---|---|
| | |
| USERNAME | USERNAME |
| PASSWORD | PASSWORD |

| WEBSITE | WEBSITE |
|---|---|
| | |
| USERNAME | USERNAME |
| PASSWORD | PASSWORD |

| WEBSITE | WEBSITE |
|---|---|
| | |
| USERNAME | USERNAME |
| PASSWORD | PASSWORD |

| WEBSITE | WEBSITE |
|---|---|
| | |
| USERNAME | USERNAME |
| PASSWORD | PASSWORD |

| WEBSITE | WEBSITE |
|---|---|
| | |
| USERNAME | USERNAME |
| PASSWORD | PASSWORD |

| WEBSITE | WEBSITE |
|---|---|
| | |
| USERNAME | USERNAME |
| PASSWORD | PASSWORD |

| WEBSITE | WEBSITE |
|---|---|
| | |
| USERNAME | USERNAME |
| PASSWORD | PASSWORD |

| WEBSITE | WEBSITE |
|---|---|
| | |
| USERNAME | USERNAME |
| PASSWORD | PASSWORD |

# PASSWORD ORGANIZER

| WEBSITE | | WEBSITE | |
|---|---|---|---|
| USERNAME | | USERNAME | |
| PASSWORD | | PASSWORD | |

| WEBSITE | | WEBSITE | |
|---|---|---|---|
| USERNAME | | USERNAME | |
| PASSWORD | | PASSWORD | |

| WEBSITE | | WEBSITE | |
|---|---|---|---|
| USERNAME | | USERNAME | |
| PASSWORD | | PASSWORD | |

| WEBSITE | | WEBSITE | |
|---|---|---|---|
| USERNAME | | USERNAME | |
| PASSWORD | | PASSWORD | |

| WEBSITE | | WEBSITE | |
|---|---|---|---|
| USERNAME | | USERNAME | |
| PASSWORD | | PASSWORD | |

| WEBSITE | | WEBSITE | |
|---|---|---|---|
| USERNAME | | USERNAME | |
| PASSWORD | | PASSWORD | |

| WEBSITE | | WEBSITE | |
|---|---|---|---|
| USERNAME | | USERNAME | |
| PASSWORD | | PASSWORD | |

| WEBSITE | | WEBSITE | |
|---|---|---|---|
| USERNAME | | USERNAME | |
| PASSWORD | | PASSWORD | |

# PASSWORD ORGANIZER

| WEBSITE | WEBSITE |
|---|---|
| | |
| USERNAME | USERNAME |
| PASSWORD | PASSWORD |

| WEBSITE | WEBSITE |
|---|---|
| | |
| USERNAME | USERNAME |
| PASSWORD | PASSWORD |

| WEBSITE | WEBSITE |
|---|---|
| | |
| USERNAME | USERNAME |
| PASSWORD | PASSWORD |

| WEBSITE | WEBSITE |
|---|---|
| | |
| USERNAME | USERNAME |
| PASSWORD | PASSWORD |

| WEBSITE | WEBSITE |
|---|---|
| | |
| USERNAME | USERNAME |
| PASSWORD | PASSWORD |

| WEBSITE | WEBSITE |
|---|---|
| | |
| USERNAME | USERNAME |
| PASSWORD | PASSWORD |

| WEBSITE | WEBSITE |
|---|---|
| | |
| USERNAME | USERNAME |
| PASSWORD | PASSWORD |

| WEBSITE | WEBSITE |
|---|---|
| | |
| USERNAME | USERNAME |
| PASSWORD | PASSWORD |

# PASSWORD ORGANIZER

| WEBSITE | WEBSITE |
|---|---|
| | |
| USERNAME | USERNAME |
| PASSWORD | PASSWORD |

| WEBSITE | WEBSITE |
|---|---|
| | |
| USERNAME | USERNAME |
| PASSWORD | PASSWORD |

| WEBSITE | WEBSITE |
|---|---|
| | |
| USERNAME | USERNAME |
| PASSWORD | PASSWORD |

| WEBSITE | WEBSITE |
|---|---|
| | |
| USERNAME | USERNAME |
| PASSWORD | PASSWORD |

| WEBSITE | WEBSITE |
|---|---|
| | |
| USERNAME | USERNAME |
| PASSWORD | PASSWORD |

| WEBSITE | WEBSITE |
|---|---|
| | |
| USERNAME | USERNAME |
| PASSWORD | PASSWORD |

| WEBSITE | WEBSITE |
|---|---|
| | |
| USERNAME | USERNAME |
| PASSWORD | PASSWORD |

| WEBSITE | WEBSITE |
|---|---|
| | |
| USERNAME | USERNAME |
| PASSWORD | PASSWORD |

# PASSWORD ORGANIZER

| WEBSITE | | WEBSITE | |
|---|---|---|---|
| USERNAME | | USERNAME | |
| PASSWORD | | PASSWORD | |

| WEBSITE | | WEBSITE | |
|---|---|---|---|
| USERNAME | | USERNAME | |
| PASSWORD | | PASSWORD | |

| WEBSITE | | WEBSITE | |
|---|---|---|---|
| USERNAME | | USERNAME | |
| PASSWORD | | PASSWORD | |

| WEBSITE | | WEBSITE | |
|---|---|---|---|
| USERNAME | | USERNAME | |
| PASSWORD | | PASSWORD | |

| WEBSITE | | WEBSITE | |
|---|---|---|---|
| USERNAME | | USERNAME | |
| PASSWORD | | PASSWORD | |

| WEBSITE | | WEBSITE | |
|---|---|---|---|
| USERNAME | | USERNAME | |
| PASSWORD | | PASSWORD | |

| WEBSITE | | WEBSITE | |
|---|---|---|---|
| USERNAME | | USERNAME | |
| PASSWORD | | PASSWORD | |

| WEBSITE | | WEBSITE | |
|---|---|---|---|
| USERNAME | | USERNAME | |
| PASSWORD | | PASSWORD | |

# PASSWORD ORGANIZER

| WEBSITE | | WEBSITE | |
|---|---|---|---|
| | | | |
| USERNAME | | USERNAME | |
| PASSWORD | | PASSWORD | |

| WEBSITE | | WEBSITE | |
|---|---|---|---|
| | | | |
| USERNAME | | USERNAME | |
| PASSWORD | | PASSWORD | |

| WEBSITE | | WEBSITE | |
|---|---|---|---|
| | | | |
| USERNAME | | USERNAME | |
| PASSWORD | | PASSWORD | |

| WEBSITE | | WEBSITE | |
|---|---|---|---|
| | | | |
| USERNAME | | USERNAME | |
| PASSWORD | | PASSWORD | |

| WEBSITE | | WEBSITE | |
|---|---|---|---|
| | | | |
| USERNAME | | USERNAME | |
| PASSWORD | | PASSWORD | |

| WEBSITE | | WEBSITE | |
|---|---|---|---|
| | | | |
| USERNAME | | USERNAME | |
| PASSWORD | | PASSWORD | |

| WEBSITE | | WEBSITE | |
|---|---|---|---|
| | | | |
| USERNAME | | USERNAME | |
| PASSWORD | | PASSWORD | |

| WEBSITE | | WEBSITE | |
|---|---|---|---|
| | | | |
| USERNAME | | USERNAME | |
| PASSWORD | | PASSWORD | |

# PASSWORD ORGANIZER

| WEBSITE | WEBSITE |
|---|---|
| | |
| USERNAME | USERNAME |
| PASSWORD | PASSWORD |

| WEBSITE | WEBSITE |
|---|---|
| | |
| USERNAME | USERNAME |
| PASSWORD | PASSWORD |

| WEBSITE | WEBSITE |
|---|---|
| | |
| USERNAME | USERNAME |
| PASSWORD | PASSWORD |

| WEBSITE | WEBSITE |
|---|---|
| | |
| USERNAME | USERNAME |
| PASSWORD | PASSWORD |

| WEBSITE | WEBSITE |
|---|---|
| | |
| USERNAME | USERNAME |
| PASSWORD | PASSWORD |

| WEBSITE | WEBSITE |
|---|---|
| | |
| USERNAME | USERNAME |
| PASSWORD | PASSWORD |

| WEBSITE | WEBSITE |
|---|---|
| | |
| USERNAME | USERNAME |
| PASSWORD | PASSWORD |

| WEBSITE | WEBSITE |
|---|---|
| | |
| USERNAME | USERNAME |
| PASSWORD | PASSWORD |

# PASSWORD ORGANIZER

| WEBSITE | | WEBSITE | |
|---|---|---|---|
| | | | |
| USERNAME | | USERNAME | |
| PASSWORD | | PASSWORD | |

| WEBSITE | | WEBSITE | |
|---|---|---|---|
| | | | |
| USERNAME | | USERNAME | |
| PASSWORD | | PASSWORD | |

| WEBSITE | | WEBSITE | |
|---|---|---|---|
| | | | |
| USERNAME | | USERNAME | |
| PASSWORD | | PASSWORD | |

| WEBSITE | | WEBSITE | |
|---|---|---|---|
| | | | |
| USERNAME | | USERNAME | |
| PASSWORD | | PASSWORD | |

| WEBSITE | | WEBSITE | |
|---|---|---|---|
| | | | |
| USERNAME | | USERNAME | |
| PASSWORD | | PASSWORD | |

| WEBSITE | | WEBSITE | |
|---|---|---|---|
| | | | |
| USERNAME | | USERNAME | |
| PASSWORD | | PASSWORD | |

| WEBSITE | | WEBSITE | |
|---|---|---|---|
| | | | |
| USERNAME | | USERNAME | |
| PASSWORD | | PASSWORD | |

| WEBSITE | | WEBSITE | |
|---|---|---|---|
| | | | |
| USERNAME | | USERNAME | |
| PASSWORD | | PASSWORD | |

# PASSWORD ORGANIZER

| WEBSITE | WEBSITE |
|---|---|
| | |
| USERNAME | USERNAME |
| PASSWORD | PASSWORD |

| WEBSITE | WEBSITE |
|---|---|
| | |
| USERNAME | USERNAME |
| PASSWORD | PASSWORD |

| WEBSITE | WEBSITE |
|---|---|
| | |
| USERNAME | USERNAME |
| PASSWORD | PASSWORD |

| WEBSITE | WEBSITE |
|---|---|
| | |
| USERNAME | USERNAME |
| PASSWORD | PASSWORD |

| WEBSITE | WEBSITE |
|---|---|
| | |
| USERNAME | USERNAME |
| PASSWORD | PASSWORD |

| WEBSITE | WEBSITE |
|---|---|
| | |
| USERNAME | USERNAME |
| PASSWORD | PASSWORD |

| WEBSITE | WEBSITE |
|---|---|
| | |
| USERNAME | USERNAME |
| PASSWORD | PASSWORD |

| WEBSITE | WEBSITE |
|---|---|
| | |
| USERNAME | USERNAME |
| PASSWORD | PASSWORD |

# PASSWORD ORGANIZER

| WEBSITE | | WEBSITE | |
|---|---|---|---|
| | | | |
| USERNAME | | USERNAME | |
| PASSWORD | | PASSWORD | |

| WEBSITE | | WEBSITE | |
|---|---|---|---|
| | | | |
| USERNAME | | USERNAME | |
| PASSWORD | | PASSWORD | |

| WEBSITE | | WEBSITE | |
|---|---|---|---|
| | | | |
| USERNAME | | USERNAME | |
| PASSWORD | | PASSWORD | |

| WEBSITE | | WEBSITE | |
|---|---|---|---|
| | | | |
| USERNAME | | USERNAME | |
| PASSWORD | | PASSWORD | |

| WEBSITE | | WEBSITE | |
|---|---|---|---|
| | | | |
| USERNAME | | USERNAME | |
| PASSWORD | | PASSWORD | |

| WEBSITE | | WEBSITE | |
|---|---|---|---|
| | | | |
| USERNAME | | USERNAME | |
| PASSWORD | | PASSWORD | |

| WEBSITE | | WEBSITE | |
|---|---|---|---|
| | | | |
| USERNAME | | USERNAME | |
| PASSWORD | | PASSWORD | |

| WEBSITE | | WEBSITE | |
|---|---|---|---|
| | | | |
| USERNAME | | USERNAME | |
| PASSWORD | | PASSWORD | |

# PASSWORD ORGANIZER

| WEBSITE | | WEBSITE | |
|---|---|---|---|
| | | | |
| USERNAME | | USERNAME | |
| PASSWORD | | PASSWORD | |

| WEBSITE | | WEBSITE | |
|---|---|---|---|
| | | | |
| USERNAME | | USERNAME | |
| PASSWORD | | PASSWORD | |

| WEBSITE | | WEBSITE | |
|---|---|---|---|
| | | | |
| USERNAME | | USERNAME | |
| PASSWORD | | PASSWORD | |

| WEBSITE | | WEBSITE | |
|---|---|---|---|
| | | | |
| USERNAME | | USERNAME | |
| PASSWORD | | PASSWORD | |

| WEBSITE | | WEBSITE | |
|---|---|---|---|
| | | | |
| USERNAME | | USERNAME | |
| PASSWORD | | PASSWORD | |

| WEBSITE | | WEBSITE | |
|---|---|---|---|
| | | | |
| USERNAME | | USERNAME | |
| PASSWORD | | PASSWORD | |

| WEBSITE | | WEBSITE | |
|---|---|---|---|
| | | | |
| USERNAME | | USERNAME | |
| PASSWORD | | PASSWORD | |

| WEBSITE | | WEBSITE | |
|---|---|---|---|
| | | | |
| USERNAME | | USERNAME | |
| PASSWORD | | PASSWORD | |

# PASSWORD ORGANIZER

| WEBSITE | WEBSITE |
|---|---|
| USERNAME | USERNAME |
| PASSWORD | PASSWORD |

| WEBSITE | WEBSITE |
|---|---|
| USERNAME | USERNAME |
| PASSWORD | PASSWORD |

| WEBSITE | WEBSITE |
|---|---|
| USERNAME | USERNAME |
| PASSWORD | PASSWORD |

| WEBSITE | WEBSITE |
|---|---|
| USERNAME | USERNAME |
| PASSWORD | PASSWORD |

| WEBSITE | WEBSITE |
|---|---|
| USERNAME | USERNAME |
| PASSWORD | PASSWORD |

| WEBSITE | WEBSITE |
|---|---|
| USERNAME | USERNAME |
| PASSWORD | PASSWORD |

| WEBSITE | WEBSITE |
|---|---|
| USERNAME | USERNAME |
| PASSWORD | PASSWORD |

| WEBSITE | WEBSITE |
|---|---|
| USERNAME | USERNAME |
| PASSWORD | PASSWORD |

# PASSWORD ORGANIZER

| WEBSITE | WEBSITE |
|---|---|
| | |
| USERNAME | USERNAME |
| PASSWORD | PASSWORD |

| WEBSITE | WEBSITE |
|---|---|
| | |
| USERNAME | USERNAME |
| PASSWORD | PASSWORD |

| WEBSITE | WEBSITE |
|---|---|
| | |
| USERNAME | USERNAME |
| PASSWORD | PASSWORD |

| WEBSITE | WEBSITE |
|---|---|
| | |
| USERNAME | USERNAME |
| PASSWORD | PASSWORD |

| WEBSITE | WEBSITE |
|---|---|
| | |
| USERNAME | USERNAME |
| PASSWORD | PASSWORD |

| WEBSITE | WEBSITE |
|---|---|
| | |
| USERNAME | USERNAME |
| PASSWORD | PASSWORD |

| WEBSITE | WEBSITE |
|---|---|
| | |
| USERNAME | USERNAME |
| PASSWORD | PASSWORD |

| WEBSITE | WEBSITE |
|---|---|
| | |
| USERNAME | USERNAME |
| PASSWORD | PASSWORD |

# PASSWORD ORGANIZER

| WEBSITE | | WEBSITE | |
|---|---|---|---|
| | | | |
| USERNAME | | USERNAME | |
| PASSWORD | | PASSWORD | |

| WEBSITE | | WEBSITE | |
|---|---|---|---|
| | | | |
| USERNAME | | USERNAME | |
| PASSWORD | | PASSWORD | |

| WEBSITE | | WEBSITE | |
|---|---|---|---|
| | | | |
| USERNAME | | USERNAME | |
| PASSWORD | | PASSWORD | |

| WEBSITE | | WEBSITE | |
|---|---|---|---|
| | | | |
| USERNAME | | USERNAME | |
| PASSWORD | | PASSWORD | |

| WEBSITE | | WEBSITE | |
|---|---|---|---|
| | | | |
| USERNAME | | USERNAME | |
| PASSWORD | | PASSWORD | |

| WEBSITE | | WEBSITE | |
|---|---|---|---|
| | | | |
| USERNAME | | USERNAME | |
| PASSWORD | | PASSWORD | |

| WEBSITE | | WEBSITE | |
|---|---|---|---|
| | | | |
| USERNAME | | USERNAME | |
| PASSWORD | | PASSWORD | |

| WEBSITE | | WEBSITE | |
|---|---|---|---|
| | | | |
| USERNAME | | USERNAME | |
| PASSWORD | | PASSWORD | |

# PASSWORD ORGANIZER

| WEBSITE | | WEBSITE | |
|---|---|---|---|
| | | | |
| USERNAME | | USERNAME | |
| PASSWORD | | PASSWORD | |

| WEBSITE | | WEBSITE | |
|---|---|---|---|
| | | | |
| USERNAME | | USERNAME | |
| PASSWORD | | PASSWORD | |

| WEBSITE | | WEBSITE | |
|---|---|---|---|
| | | | |
| USERNAME | | USERNAME | |
| PASSWORD | | PASSWORD | |

| WEBSITE | | WEBSITE | |
|---|---|---|---|
| | | | |
| USERNAME | | USERNAME | |
| PASSWORD | | PASSWORD | |

| WEBSITE | | WEBSITE | |
|---|---|---|---|
| | | | |
| USERNAME | | USERNAME | |
| PASSWORD | | PASSWORD | |

| WEBSITE | | WEBSITE | |
|---|---|---|---|
| | | | |
| USERNAME | | USERNAME | |
| PASSWORD | | PASSWORD | |

| WEBSITE | | WEBSITE | |
|---|---|---|---|
| | | | |
| USERNAME | | USERNAME | |
| PASSWORD | | PASSWORD | |

| WEBSITE | | WEBSITE | |
|---|---|---|---|
| | | | |
| USERNAME | | USERNAME | |
| PASSWORD | | PASSWORD | |

# PASSWORD ORGANIZER

| WEBSITE | WEBSITE |
|---|---|
| | |
| USERNAME | USERNAME |
| PASSWORD | PASSWORD |

| WEBSITE | WEBSITE |
|---|---|
| | |
| USERNAME | USERNAME |
| PASSWORD | PASSWORD |

| WEBSITE | WEBSITE |
|---|---|
| | |
| USERNAME | USERNAME |
| PASSWORD | PASSWORD |

| WEBSITE | WEBSITE |
|---|---|
| | |
| USERNAME | USERNAME |
| PASSWORD | PASSWORD |

| WEBSITE | WEBSITE |
|---|---|
| | |
| USERNAME | USERNAME |
| PASSWORD | PASSWORD |

| WEBSITE | WEBSITE |
|---|---|
| | |
| USERNAME | USERNAME |
| PASSWORD | PASSWORD |

| WEBSITE | WEBSITE |
|---|---|
| | |
| USERNAME | USERNAME |
| PASSWORD | PASSWORD |

| WEBSITE | WEBSITE |
|---|---|
| | |
| USERNAME | USERNAME |
| PASSWORD | PASSWORD |

# PASSWORD ORGANIZER

| WEBSITE | | WEBSITE |
|---|---|---|
| | | |
| USERNAME | | USERNAME |
| PASSWORD | | PASSWORD |

| WEBSITE | | WEBSITE |
|---|---|---|
| | | |
| USERNAME | | USERNAME |
| PASSWORD | | PASSWORD |

| WEBSITE | | WEBSITE |
|---|---|---|
| | | |
| USERNAME | | USERNAME |
| PASSWORD | | PASSWORD |

| WEBSITE | | WEBSITE |
|---|---|---|
| | | |
| USERNAME | | USERNAME |
| PASSWORD | | PASSWORD |

| WEBSITE | | WEBSITE |
|---|---|---|
| | | |
| USERNAME | | USERNAME |
| PASSWORD | | PASSWORD |

| WEBSITE | | WEBSITE |
|---|---|---|
| | | |
| USERNAME | | USERNAME |
| PASSWORD | | PASSWORD |

| WEBSITE | | WEBSITE |
|---|---|---|
| | | |
| USERNAME | | USERNAME |
| PASSWORD | | PASSWORD |

| WEBSITE | | WEBSITE |
|---|---|---|
| | | |
| USERNAME | | USERNAME |
| PASSWORD | | PASSWORD |

# PASSWORD ORGANIZER

| WEBSITE | | WEBSITE | |
|---|---|---|---|
| | | | |
| USERNAME | | USERNAME | |
| PASSWORD | | PASSWORD | |

| WEBSITE | | WEBSITE | |
|---|---|---|---|
| | | | |
| USERNAME | | USERNAME | |
| PASSWORD | | PASSWORD | |

| WEBSITE | | WEBSITE | |
|---|---|---|---|
| | | | |
| USERNAME | | USERNAME | |
| PASSWORD | | PASSWORD | |

| WEBSITE | | WEBSITE | |
|---|---|---|---|
| | | | |
| USERNAME | | USERNAME | |
| PASSWORD | | PASSWORD | |

| WEBSITE | | WEBSITE | |
|---|---|---|---|
| | | | |
| USERNAME | | USERNAME | |
| PASSWORD | | PASSWORD | |

| WEBSITE | | WEBSITE | |
|---|---|---|---|
| | | | |
| USERNAME | | USERNAME | |
| PASSWORD | | PASSWORD | |

| WEBSITE | | WEBSITE | |
|---|---|---|---|
| | | | |
| USERNAME | | USERNAME | |
| PASSWORD | | PASSWORD | |

| WEBSITE | | WEBSITE | |
|---|---|---|---|
| | | | |
| USERNAME | | USERNAME | |
| PASSWORD | | PASSWORD | |

# PASSWORD ORGANIZER

| WEBSITE | | WEBSITE |
|---|---|---|
| | | |
| USERNAME | | USERNAME |
| PASSWORD | | PASSWORD |

| WEBSITE | | WEBSITE |
|---|---|---|
| | | |
| USERNAME | | USERNAME |
| PASSWORD | | PASSWORD |

| WEBSITE | | WEBSITE |
|---|---|---|
| | | |
| USERNAME | | USERNAME |
| PASSWORD | | PASSWORD |

| WEBSITE | | WEBSITE |
|---|---|---|
| | | |
| USERNAME | | USERNAME |
| PASSWORD | | PASSWORD |

| WEBSITE | | WEBSITE |
|---|---|---|
| | | |
| USERNAME | | USERNAME |
| PASSWORD | | PASSWORD |

| WEBSITE | | WEBSITE |
|---|---|---|
| | | |
| USERNAME | | USERNAME |
| PASSWORD | | PASSWORD |

| WEBSITE | | WEBSITE |
|---|---|---|
| | | |
| USERNAME | | USERNAME |
| PASSWORD | | PASSWORD |

| WEBSITE | | WEBSITE |
|---|---|---|
| | | |
| USERNAME | | USERNAME |
| PASSWORD | | PASSWORD |

# PASSWORD ORGANIZER

| WEBSITE | | WEBSITE |
|---|---|---|
| | | |
| USERNAME | | USERNAME |
| PASSWORD | | PASSWORD |

| WEBSITE | | WEBSITE |
|---|---|---|
| | | |
| USERNAME | | USERNAME |
| PASSWORD | | PASSWORD |

| WEBSITE | | WEBSITE |
|---|---|---|
| | | |
| USERNAME | | USERNAME |
| PASSWORD | | PASSWORD |

| WEBSITE | | WEBSITE |
|---|---|---|
| | | |
| USERNAME | | USERNAME |
| PASSWORD | | PASSWORD |

| WEBSITE | | WEBSITE |
|---|---|---|
| | | |
| USERNAME | | USERNAME |
| PASSWORD | | PASSWORD |

| WEBSITE | | WEBSITE |
|---|---|---|
| | | |
| USERNAME | | USERNAME |
| PASSWORD | | PASSWORD |

| WEBSITE | | WEBSITE |
|---|---|---|
| | | |
| USERNAME | | USERNAME |
| PASSWORD | | PASSWORD |

| WEBSITE | | WEBSITE |
|---|---|---|
| | | |
| USERNAME | | USERNAME |
| PASSWORD | | PASSWORD |

# PASSWORD ORGANIZER

| WEBSITE | WEBSITE |
|---|---|
| | |
| USERNAME | USERNAME |
| PASSWORD | PASSWORD |

| WEBSITE | WEBSITE |
|---|---|
| | |
| USERNAME | USERNAME |
| PASSWORD | PASSWORD |

| WEBSITE | WEBSITE |
|---|---|
| | |
| USERNAME | USERNAME |
| PASSWORD | PASSWORD |

| WEBSITE | WEBSITE |
|---|---|
| | |
| USERNAME | USERNAME |
| PASSWORD | PASSWORD |

| WEBSITE | WEBSITE |
|---|---|
| | |
| USERNAME | USERNAME |
| PASSWORD | PASSWORD |

| WEBSITE | WEBSITE |
|---|---|
| | |
| USERNAME | USERNAME |
| PASSWORD | PASSWORD |

| WEBSITE | WEBSITE |
|---|---|
| | |
| USERNAME | USERNAME |
| PASSWORD | PASSWORD |

| WEBSITE | WEBSITE |
|---|---|
| | |
| USERNAME | USERNAME |
| PASSWORD | PASSWORD |

# PASSWORD ORGANIZER

| WEBSITE | WEBSITE |
|---|---|
| USERNAME | USERNAME |
| PASSWORD | PASSWORD |

| WEBSITE | WEBSITE |
|---|---|
| USERNAME | USERNAME |
| PASSWORD | PASSWORD |

| WEBSITE | WEBSITE |
|---|---|
| USERNAME | USERNAME |
| PASSWORD | PASSWORD |

| WEBSITE | WEBSITE |
|---|---|
| USERNAME | USERNAME |
| PASSWORD | PASSWORD |

| WEBSITE | WEBSITE |
|---|---|
| USERNAME | USERNAME |
| PASSWORD | PASSWORD |

| WEBSITE | WEBSITE |
|---|---|
| USERNAME | USERNAME |
| PASSWORD | PASSWORD |

| WEBSITE | WEBSITE |
|---|---|
| USERNAME | USERNAME |
| PASSWORD | PASSWORD |

| WEBSITE | WEBSITE |
|---|---|
| USERNAME | USERNAME |
| PASSWORD | PASSWORD |

# PASSWORD ORGANIZER

| WEBSITE | WEBSITE |
|---|---|
| | |
| USERNAME | USERNAME |
| PASSWORD | PASSWORD |

| WEBSITE | WEBSITE |
|---|---|
| | |
| USERNAME | USERNAME |
| PASSWORD | PASSWORD |

| WEBSITE | WEBSITE |
|---|---|
| | |
| USERNAME | USERNAME |
| PASSWORD | PASSWORD |

| WEBSITE | WEBSITE |
|---|---|
| | |
| USERNAME | USERNAME |
| PASSWORD | PASSWORD |

| WEBSITE | WEBSITE |
|---|---|
| | |
| USERNAME | USERNAME |
| PASSWORD | PASSWORD |

| WEBSITE | WEBSITE |
|---|---|
| | |
| USERNAME | USERNAME |
| PASSWORD | PASSWORD |

| WEBSITE | WEBSITE |
|---|---|
| | |
| USERNAME | USERNAME |
| PASSWORD | PASSWORD |

| WEBSITE | WEBSITE |
|---|---|
| | |
| USERNAME | USERNAME |
| PASSWORD | PASSWORD |

# PASSWORD ORGANIZER

| WEBSITE | WEBSITE |
|---|---|
| | |
| USERNAME | USERNAME |
| PASSWORD | PASSWORD |

| WEBSITE | WEBSITE |
|---|---|
| | |
| USERNAME | USERNAME |
| PASSWORD | PASSWORD |

| WEBSITE | WEBSITE |
|---|---|
| | |
| USERNAME | USERNAME |
| PASSWORD | PASSWORD |

| WEBSITE | WEBSITE |
|---|---|
| | |
| USERNAME | USERNAME |
| PASSWORD | PASSWORD |

| WEBSITE | WEBSITE |
|---|---|
| | |
| USERNAME | USERNAME |
| PASSWORD | PASSWORD |

| WEBSITE | WEBSITE |
|---|---|
| | |
| USERNAME | USERNAME |
| PASSWORD | PASSWORD |

| WEBSITE | WEBSITE |
|---|---|
| | |
| USERNAME | USERNAME |
| PASSWORD | PASSWORD |

| WEBSITE | WEBSITE |
|---|---|
| | |
| USERNAME | USERNAME |
| PASSWORD | PASSWORD |

# PASSWORD ORGANIZER

| WEBSITE |
|---|
| |
| USERNAME |
| PASSWORD |

| WEBSITE |
|---|
| |
| USERNAME |
| PASSWORD |

| WEBSITE |
|---|
| |
| USERNAME |
| PASSWORD |

| WEBSITE |
|---|
| |
| USERNAME |
| PASSWORD |

| WEBSITE |
|---|
| |
| USERNAME |
| PASSWORD |

| WEBSITE |
|---|
| |
| USERNAME |
| PASSWORD |

| WEBSITE |
|---|
| |
| USERNAME |
| PASSWORD |

| WEBSITE |
|---|
| |
| USERNAME |
| PASSWORD |

| WEBSITE |
|---|
| |
| USERNAME |
| PASSWORD |

| WEBSITE |
|---|
| |
| USERNAME |
| PASSWORD |

| WEBSITE |
|---|
| |
| USERNAME |
| PASSWORD |

| WEBSITE |
|---|
| |
| USERNAME |
| PASSWORD |

| WEBSITE |
|---|
| |
| USERNAME |
| PASSWORD |

| WEBSITE |
|---|
| |
| USERNAME |
| PASSWORD |

| WEBSITE |
|---|
| |
| USERNAME |
| PASSWORD |

| WEBSITE |
|---|
| |
| USERNAME |
| PASSWORD |

# PASSWORD ORGANIZER

| WEBSITE | WEBSITE |
|---|---|
| | |
| USERNAME | USERNAME |
| PASSWORD | PASSWORD |

| WEBSITE | WEBSITE |
|---|---|
| | |
| USERNAME | USERNAME |
| PASSWORD | PASSWORD |

| WEBSITE | WEBSITE |
|---|---|
| | |
| USERNAME | USERNAME |
| PASSWORD | PASSWORD |

| WEBSITE | WEBSITE |
|---|---|
| | |
| USERNAME | USERNAME |
| PASSWORD | PASSWORD |

| WEBSITE | WEBSITE |
|---|---|
| | |
| USERNAME | USERNAME |
| PASSWORD | PASSWORD |

| WEBSITE | WEBSITE |
|---|---|
| | |
| USERNAME | USERNAME |
| PASSWORD | PASSWORD |

| WEBSITE | WEBSITE |
|---|---|
| | |
| USERNAME | USERNAME |
| PASSWORD | PASSWORD |

| WEBSITE | WEBSITE |
|---|---|
| | |
| USERNAME | USERNAME |
| PASSWORD | PASSWORD |

# PASSWORD ORGANIZER

| WEBSITE |
|---|
|  |
| USERNAME |
| PASSWORD |

| WEBSITE |
|---|
|  |
| USERNAME |
| PASSWORD |

| WEBSITE |
|---|
|  |
| USERNAME |
| PASSWORD |

| WEBSITE |
|---|
|  |
| USERNAME |
| PASSWORD |

| WEBSITE |
|---|
|  |
| USERNAME |
| PASSWORD |

| WEBSITE |
|---|
|  |
| USERNAME |
| PASSWORD |

| WEBSITE |
|---|
|  |
| USERNAME |
| PASSWORD |

| WEBSITE |
|---|
|  |
| USERNAME |
| PASSWORD |

| WEBSITE |
|---|
|  |
| USERNAME |
| PASSWORD |

| WEBSITE |
|---|
|  |
| USERNAME |
| PASSWORD |

| WEBSITE |
|---|
|  |
| USERNAME |
| PASSWORD |

| WEBSITE |
|---|
|  |
| USERNAME |
| PASSWORD |

| WEBSITE |
|---|
|  |
| USERNAME |
| PASSWORD |

| WEBSITE |
|---|
|  |
| USERNAME |
| PASSWORD |

| WEBSITE |
|---|
|  |
| USERNAME |
| PASSWORD |

| WEBSITE |
|---|
|  |
| USERNAME |
| PASSWORD |

www.ingramcontent.com/pod-product-compliance
Lightning Source LLC
Chambersburg PA
CBHW060444060326
40690CB00019B/4332